1 6 4

5 2 8

3 9

11 7 22

THE PREDICTIONS LIBRARY

NUMEROLOGY

David V. Barrett

1 9 5 6 3 4
11 2 8 7 22

DORLING KINDERSLEY
London · New York · Stuttgart

A DORLING KINDERSLEY BOOK

Senior Editor • Sharon Lucas
Art Editor • Anna Benjamin
Managing Editor • Krystyna Mayer
Managing Art Editor • Derek Coombes
DTP Designer • Cressida Joyce
Picture Researcher • Becky Halls
Production Controller • Sarah Fuller
US Editor • Connie Mersel

First American Edition, 1995
2 4 6 8 10 9 7 5 3 1

Published in the United States by Dorling Kindersley Publishing, Inc.,
95 Madison Avenue, New York, New York 10016

Distributed by Houghton Mifflin Company, Boston.

Library of Congress Cataloging-in-Publication Data

Barrett, David V.
  Numerology / by David V. Barrett. -- 1st American ed.
    p.   cm. -- (The predictions library)
  ISBN 0-7894-0307-2
  1. Numerology.   I. Title.   II. Series: Barrett, David V.
Predictions library.
BF1623.P9B394   1995
133 . 3 '35--dc20   95-11680
                                                              CIP

Reproduced by Bright Arts, Hong Kong
Printed and bound in Hong Kong by Imago

CONTENTS

Introducing Numerology 8

History of Numerology 10

Pythagoras 12

The Basics of
Numerology 14

The Meanings of Numbers:
One & Two 16

Three & Four 18

Five & Six 20

Seven & Eight 22

Nine, Eleven, &
Twenty-Two 24

Your Date of Birth
Number 26

Your Birthday Number 28

The Arrows of Pythagoras 30

Interpreting the Arrows
of Pythagoras 32

Turning your Name into a
Number 34

Your Vowel Number 36

Your Consonant Number   38

Your Whole Name
Number 40

Your Name & the Arrows
of Pythagoras 42

Putting your Date
& Name Together 44

Missing Numbers 46

Changing your Name 48

The Numerology of Years 50

Other Uses of Numbers:
Squares 52

Other Uses of Numbers:
Esoteric Systems 54

Other Uses of Numbers:
Music 56

Other Uses of Numbers:
Colors 58

Index & Credits 60

INTRODUCING
NUMEROLOGY

NUMEROLOGY IS THE STUDY OF THE ESOTERIC
SIGNIFICANCE OF NUMBERS AND OF ANYTHING THAT
CAN BE CONVERTED INTO NUMBERS, ESPECIALLY YOUR
DATE OF BIRTH AND YOUR NAME.

Numbers have always had religious and magical significance. The Old Testament gives the precise dimensions of Noah's Ark and of the various parts of Solomon's Temple. Similarly, many medieval cathedrals were designed and constructed to geometric patterns with powerful esoteric significance. The Freemasons and Rosicrucians still hold the secrets of architectural magic.

Names also have religious and magical importance, and all names have an original meaning. For example, Anna is the Greek form of the Hebrew name Hannah, which means "God has favored me." Christine,

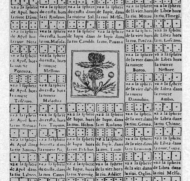

DIVINE DICE
Dice have been used for divination since ancient times. This 16th-century French sheet is for a game based on the fall of the dice, and was used to obtain responses to questions about the future.

SACRED TWELVE
This 14th-century French miniature shows the sacred number 12, which is the number of the prophets and the apostles.

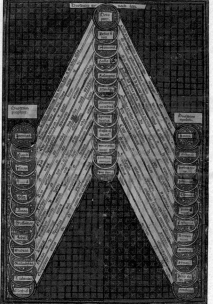

Krystyna, and all the other variants of the name simply mean "Christian." The name David is from the Hebrew for "beloved" or "friend." Derek, Dietrich, and Thierry all originate from Theodoric, meaning "ruler of the people." Sharon refers to the fertile coastal plain of Palestine.

Names also have significant power. In many societies it has been considered dangerous to let a stranger know your name, in case the stranger decided to lay a curse on you. One way of avoiding this problem was to have a secret name, known only to yourself. Any other "known" name would then only be a public label, rather than containing the essence of your identity.

Names can also be converted to numbers. In numerology, it is not the original meaning of a name that is significant, but the sum of the numerical equivalent of each of its letters. Numerologists believe that the number your name can be reduced to contains vital information about your personality and the goals you should strive for in life.

HISTORY
of NUMEROLOGY

NUMBERS HAVE BEEN IMPORTANT WHEREVER
CIVILIZATION, RELIGION, THE ARTS, AND SCIENCE HAVE
EXISTED. NUMBERS HAVE BEEN USED FOR COUNTING,
DESIGNING BUILDINGS, AND MYSTICAL PURPOSES.

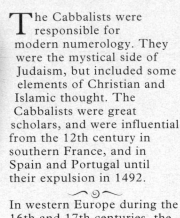

The Cabbalists were responsible for modern numerology. They were the mystical side of Judaism, but included some elements of Christian and Islamic thought. The Cabbalists were great scholars, and were influential from the 12th century in southern France, and in Spain and Portugal until their expulsion in 1492.

In western Europe during the 16th and 17th centuries, the Hermetic philosophers studied and practiced

TREE OF LIFE
*This 17th-century Tree of Life,
also known as the Sephirothic
Tree, is part of the Cabbalah's
complex diagrammatic system
that illustrates the relationship
between God and man.*

MAGIC MAN
This woodcut of Henry Cornelius Agrippa of Netterheim is from his work, De Occulta Philosophia, *1533. He was an occultist, Hermetic philosopher, and magician.*

astrology, alchemy, magic, and the mystical significance of numbers. This movement included Henry Cornelius Agrippa (1486–1535), John Dee (1527–1608), Robert Fludd (1574–1637), and Elias Ashmole (1617–92). In some ways, they could be considered the Christian equivalent of the Cabbalists.

~ ⌒ ~

In the 19th and early 20th centuries, numerology became little more than an entertaining parlor game, but eventually the subject was formalized scientifically. Many contemporary numerological systems stem from the teachings of the American numcrologist L. Dow Balliett (1847–1929) and the California Institute of Numerical Research, which was founded by Balliett student Dr. Juno Jordan. In recent years, the widespread New Age revival has started to bring numerology back toward its symbolic and mystical roots.

PYTHAGORAS

THE FAMOUS PHILOSOPHER AND MATHEMATICIAN,
PYTHAGORAS, WAS FASCINATED BY THE STARS, THE
"MUSIC OF THE SPHERES," AND THE RELATIONSHIPS
BETWEEN NUMBERS. HE IS CONSIDERED TO BE
ONE OF THE FOUNDERS OF NUMEROLOGY.

Pythagoras (*c.* 580–500 BC) is probably best known for his theorem about the sides of a right-angled triangle. The geometrical properties of triangles and squares continually fascinated Pythagoras. His theorem was only one calculation in a huge body of work, which included a lifetime study of the significance of numbers in geometry, music, architecture, astrology, and astronomy.

~ ૭ ~

Pythagoras traveled around the ancient world for many years, learning about the

WHO WAS HE?
Pythagoras was the founder of the influential religious brotherhood, the Pythagoreans. They believed in immortality and in the transmigration of souls, which is also known as reincarnation.

SACRED SPACE
This image shows an overhead view of the galaxy, but when Pythagoras studied astronomy and astrology, he observed "the worlds moving through space in accordance with the rhythm and harmony of the sacred numbers."

universe, humankind, and God from the many religions, philosophies, and sciences that he encountered. He incorporated everything that he learned into one system and established an esoteric school in Crotona in southern Italy, where he passed on his teachings to carefully selected students. Later philosophers such as Plato (*c.* 428–*c.* 348 BC) and Aristotle (384–322 BC) built on his work.

For Pythagoras and the influential Pythagorean school of thought, numbers could be found behind every area of life. Pythagoras is credited with discovering the mathematical relationships between musical notes, including the octave, and the intervals between musical notes that make harmonies.

According to Pythagoras, odd numbers were male, active, and creative; even numbers were female, passive, and receptive. Each number from one to nine had its own specific properties, and Pythagoras's description of these properties is still a major influence on modern-day numerology.

THE BASICS *of*
NUMEROLOGY

NUMEROLOGY TAKES YOUR NAME AND DATE OF BIRTH,
AND REDUCES THESE IN A VARIETY OF WAYS TO SINGLE
DIGITS. THE RESULTANT NUMBERS ARE BELIEVED TO
REVEAL YOUR PERSONALITY.

Although numerology reduces your name and date of birth to single digits in order to reveal

MALE NUMBERS
Michelangelo's "David" is considered to be one of the most perfect examples of masculinity in art. In numerology, odd numbers are masculine.

your essential self, your strengths and weaknesses, and the goals that you should try to achieve in life, very few people are likely to be completely one number. Your personality is more likely to contain elements of several numbers. In numerological terms, it is the interplay between these numbers that makes up your individual, complex personality. However, many people have one number that occurs far more than the others.

Pythagoras's ancient theory about the masculinity and femininity of numbers (*see page 13*) is still widely used in modern-day numerology. Odd numbers are considered to be male, and even numbers are considered to be female.

The terms male and female, or masculine and feminine, have virtually nothing to do with your gender. Ascribing such attributes as passive, receptive, yielding, and warm to the word feminine, and active, creative, thrusting, and cold to the word masculine, is considered politically incorrect and sexist in contemporary society. Unfortunately, it is difficult to avoid this terminology in numerology, because it is a clear reflection of the relative position of men and women in past societies.

~ 9 ~

Everyone is comprised of a mixture of "masculine" and "feminine" attributes. For example, there are many men who are gentle and yielding, and many women who are aggressive and forceful.

~ 9 ~

Numerology deals mainly with the digits 1 to 9. The number 0 was a relatively late addition to mathematical notation. Although it was introduced in the ninth century by an Arab scholar, it was not accepted in Western Europe for many centuries. The number 0 has

FEMALE NUMBERS
This ancient Greek statue is the "Venus de Milo," the goddess of love. In numerology, even numbers are considered to be feminine.

no significance in numerology. The numbers 11 and 22 can sometimes be important in numerology. Both numbers have esoteric meanings of their own (*see page 25*). However, if either 11 or 22 occur as the result of a numerological calculation, it should be reduced to 2 (1+1) and 4 (2+2) respectively.

THE MEANINGS
of NUMBERS

NUMEROLOGISTS WORK WITH THE NUMBERS 1 TO 9, 11,
AND 22. THE VARIOUS MEANINGS OF THESE NUMBERS
ARE CONSIDERED TO ENCOMPASS ALL THE EXPERIENCE
THAT YOUR LIFE CAN POSSIBLY PRESENT.

ONE
This is the number of unity and beginnings, and therefore the number of God, the creator of the universe. It is also the first male number, partly because of its phallic shape and partly for its powerful creative character. It is the symbol of physical and mental activity.

~🌀~

In personality terms, this number represents leadership, organization, and ambition. People with many 1s in their numerological makeup are natural leaders. They originate ideas and have the organizational abilities to carry them through. They are likely to be individualists and are unlikely to fit in well as subordinate members of a team. They might be loners, and could be so opinionated that others may perceive them as being aggressive.

One-
humped
camel

TWO

In gnostic, dualist beliefs, the holy god was in conflict with an evil god. If 1 represents God, then 2 must represent the evil god, or the devil. However, the main characteristic of two is that of the female – yielding, receptive, accepting, and passive. In physical sexual terms, the shape of two vertical lines, as in the Roman numeral II, is considered to symbolize the vagina into which the penis-shaped I fits.

Two black cherries

The personality of people with many 2s is the direct opposite of 1. Those with many 2s are passive, and followers rather than leaders. They make very good subordinates and members of a team. However, 2-types are likely to be too subservient, and their natural gentleness might be perceived as shyness or even weakness.

They would much rather quietly persuade people to adopt their point of view than to impose it on them. They have a natural reconciliatory ability. Invariably able to appreciate both sides of an argument, they can often draw opposing sides together.

THREE

This is the generative number, partly because its shape suggests the male genitals and sexual union, but also because 1 and 2, male and female, make 3, the offspring. Geometrically, 1 is a point, 2 is a line, but 3 is the first plane figure, the triangle. A triangle pointing upward represents male sexuality and fire; a triangle pointing downward represents female sexuality and water.

Three-leaved clover

It is a holy number; there is the Christian Trinity, and triple gods in the ancient Celtic religion and Hinduism.

People with many 3s in their numerological makeup are active, harmonious, and pleasure-loving. Such people try to reconcile the opposites of 1 and 2, and seek to draw them together into the perfect and fruitful result of 3. They are extremely versatile and sociable, and tend to be sexually interested and interesting. Although 3-types make excellent conversationalists, they can sometimes be perceived as superficial.

FOUR

This is the number of matter. Quartets tend to be extremely solid and stable, and concerned with immutable constructions such as the 4 seasons, the 4 elements, and the 4 main points of the compass. The cube, with its 4-sided base, top, and sides, represents both stability and rigidity in magical geometry and architecture.

In personality numerology, 4 represents stability. Although stability is important in life, it can also be unmoving and dull. The same can be said for people with many 4s in their makeup. They tend to be hardworking, and good at their job, particularly in areas such as planning, organization, and administration, but there is unlikely to be much flair and excitement in their actions. "Inspiring" and "unconventional" rarely apply to 4s, but society could not manage without their stability.

Four-winged dragonfly

GEANE

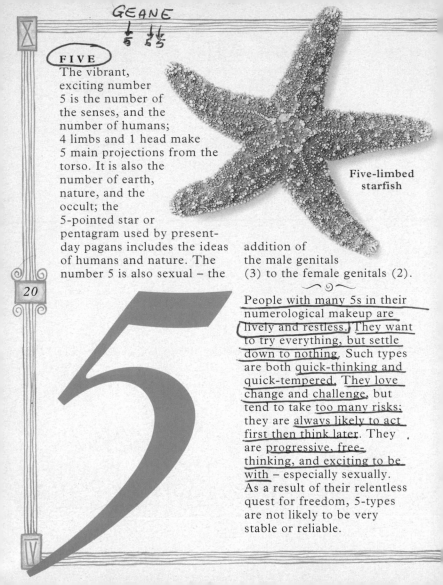

FIVE

The vibrant, exciting number 5 is the number of the senses, and the number of humans; 4 limbs and 1 head make 5 main projections from the torso. It is also the number of earth, nature, and the occult; the 5-pointed star or pentagram used by present-day pagans includes the ideas of humans and nature. The number 5 is also sexual – the addition of the male genitals (3) to the female genitals (2).

Five-limbed starfish

20

People with many 5s in their numerological makeup are lively and restless. They want to try everything, but settle down to nothing. Such types are both quick-thinking and quick-tempered. They love change and challenge, but tend to take too many risks; they are always likely to act first then think later. They are progressive, free-thinking, and exciting to be with – especially sexually. As a result of their relentless quest for freedom, 5-types are not likely to be very stable or reliable.

6

SIX
This is one of the most harmonious numbers. Mathematically it is both 2 x 3 and 1+2+3, and symbolically it is well-balanced. It is the number of Creation (6 days), and it is also the number of harmonious sexual union; the upward (male) and downward (female) triangles superimposed form the 6-pointed star. It is both a female number and 2 x 3, and can therefore represent the nurturing side of womanhood – the safe, stable, warm, domestic aspect of motherhood.

~ 9 ~

People with many 6s in their numerological makeup are natural homemakers, and love the warmth and security of the family. Such people are supportive, harmonious, and companionable. They are good at taking responsibility. Sometimes smug and self-satisfied, they may also have a tendency to interfere, believing that they always know what is best.

Number 6 toy racing car

SEVEN

This is one of the holiest and most magical of all the numbers. In the Judeo-Christian religions, God created the world in 6 days and rested on the 7th, making the week of 7 days. There are also 7 colors of the rainbow, 7 pillars of wisdom, and 7 wonders of the world.

People with many 7s in their numerological makeup are reflective, and have a tendency toward mysticism or unorthodox religion. Such people are very likely to be introspective individualists, or simply loners. Often highly intellectual, they might find it difficult to be sociable.

Consequently, they might be perceived as cold and distant. The opinions of other people are unlikely to affect 7-types too much. They plan and work extremely well on their own, and tend to be temperamentally unsuited to the camaraderie of working in a team. Worldly pursuits and pleasures hold virtually no importance for 7s, and they much prefer to enjoy the escapism of fantasies and daydreams.

The seven chakras

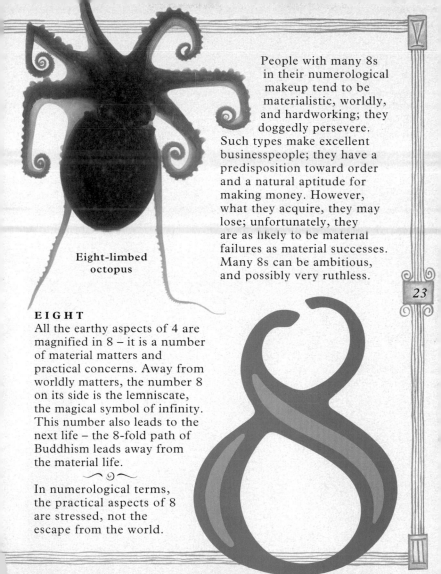

People with many 8s in their numerological makeup tend to be materialistic, worldly, and hardworking; they doggedly persevere. Such types make excellent businesspeople; they have a predisposition toward order and a natural aptitude for making money. However, what they acquire, they may lose; unfortunately, they are as likely to be material failures as material successes. Many 8s can be ambitious, and possibly very ruthless.

Eight-limbed octopus

EIGHT

All the earthy aspects of 4 are magnified in 8 – it is a number of material matters and practical concerns. Away from worldly matters, the number 8 on its side is the lemniscate, the magical symbol of infinity. This number also leads to the next life – the 8-fold path of Buddhism leads away from the material life.

In numerological terms, the practical aspects of 8 are stressed, not the escape from the world.

NINE

Because 9 is the product of 3 x 3, it is an extremely powerful number. The highest single digit, 9 represents both achievement and completion. It is associated with pregnancy, partly because of the 9 months of pregnancy, and partly because of the number's rounded, bellylike shape. Also the number of initiation, 9 represents advancing from an early state to a higher state.

People with many 9s in their numerological makeup are achievers. Such people have many bright ideas and high ideals. They pursue these with all their energy, and are not afraid to leave everyone else behind in their wake. Such types are creative, often artistic, and are well aware of their brilliance. Although 9s are proud of their abilities and love the sound of applause, they never flaunt their achievements.

Nine kittens

ELEVEN

This is the number of revelation and spiritual insight. People with many 11s in their numerological makeup rely on their intuition but are also practical. They are unconventional but sensible. Because 11 reduces to 2 (1+1), 11-type people have many 2-type attributes. However, both 1s in 11 also give 1-type qualities, and consequently, 11-type people may not be sure whether they are followers or leaders.

TWENTY-TWO

The number 22 is important in the Cabbalah. The 10 points on the Tree of Life, called Sephiroth, are joined by 22 paths, the Hebrew alphabet has 22 letters, and there are 22 cards in the Major Arcana of Tarot. It is the number of completion and perfection. People with many 22s in their numerological makeup like to control their lives and environment. Although 22 reduces to 4 (2+2), 22-type people have the more positive aspects of the number 4.

YOUR DATE *of* BIRTH
NUMBER

YOUR DATE OF BIRTH IS A HISTORICAL FACT, AND CONSEQUENTLY, CANNOT BE CHANGED. IN NUMEROLOGY, YOUR DATE OF BIRTH NUMBER IS BASED ON THE FULL DATE OF YOUR BIRTH.

Your Date of Birth number shows the best path or direction for your life. If you follow this life path, it should prove straightforward and advantageous for you. The Date of Birth number is an extremely important number, especially when considered alongside the other numbers relevant to your life. It is sometimes known as the Destiny number.

Your Date of Birth number is easy to calculate. Simply write your date of birth in numerical form and add all the digits together.

For example, John was born on February 18, 1942, so the numbers are written 2/18/1942. In Europe this date would be written 18/2/1942, with the day being put first, but this makes no difference to the calculation.

To calculate your Date of Birth number, first add the numbers of your date of birth together to form a total. Second, add the individual digits of that total together until only one digit is remaining. The example below shows how to calculate John's Date of Birth number.

$$2 + 1 + 8 + 1 + 9 + 4 + 2 = 27$$

John's Date of Birth number

$$2 + 7 = 9$$

$$1 + 1 + 2 + 3 + 1 + 9 + 7 + 5 = 29$$

$$2 + 9 = 11$$

Hannah's Date of Birth number

$$1 + 1 = 2$$

John's Date of Birth number is 9. The numerological meanings of the number 9 (*see page 24*), reveal that John has many tremendous opportunities in his life. He is a natural achiever, charismatic, and full of ideas that need to be expressed. Ideally, he should find a job or a vocation where he has the opportunity to follow this exciting life path.

~ ☙ ~

Hannah was born on November 23, 1975. In order to calculate her Date of Birth number, her date of birth would be written 11/23/1975, or 23/11/1975 in Europe. In the example above, the numbers are added together to form a total. The individual digits of that total are then added together until only one digit, the Date of Birth number, remains.

Hannah's Date of Birth calculation is interesting; the final digit is 2, but she should also examine the meaning of 11. Although 11 is the penultimate number in the calculation, it is an important number in numerology.

~ ☙ ~

The numerological meanings of the number 2 (*see page 17*) show that Hannah's life is likely to work best if she takes the role of a natural follower, rather than striving to be a leader. The numerological meanings of the number 11 (*see page 25*) show that Hannah has an intuitive, perhaps spiritual, dimension to her personality. She might be suited to social work, counseling, or the church, but in a quiet, supportive role as opposed to a more overt role as a director or evangelist.

YOUR BIRTHDAY
NUMBER

THIS NUMBER REVEALS YOUR BASIC PERSONALITY –
HOW YOU THINK AND BEHAVE. IT IS CALCULATED BY
ADDING TOGETHER, IF NECESSARY, THE DIGITS OF
THE DAY OF THE MONTH YOU WERE BORN.

The Birthday number calculation is simple. For example, John was born on February 18. Adding together the digits of the day of the month he was born gives:

$$1 + 8 = 9$$

John's Birthday number is 9, which is the same as his Date of Birth number (*see pages 26–27*). If your Birthday number is the same as your Date of Birth number, your personality and your life path can strengthen each other.

The numerological meanings of the number 9 (*see page 24*) show that John's life path is charismatic, successful, and creative. John's basic personality – how he thinks and behaves when he is unconstrained by any other factors – is revealed by his Birthday number. It shows that his personality is ideally suited to his life path. He is naturally creative and brilliant, and can carry these qualities into action.

John's life path might have been much more difficult if the numbers were not the same. For example, if John's Birthday number had been 4, the numerological meanings of the number 4 (*see page 19*) suggest that the achievement of his life path would only have been reached through determination and extremely hard work. If his Date of Birth number had been 4, his naturally creative personality might have been effectively buried in a stable but unexciting life path.

Hannah was born on November 23. In the same way as before, adding together the digits of the day of the month on which she was born gives:

$$2 + 3 = 5$$

Her Birthday number is 5, and her Date of Birth number is 2. If the Birthday and Date of Birth numbers are different, there might be conflict between the inner personality and the life path. However, it is also possible for the different aspects of the two numbers to resolve the potential weaknesses in each other.

~ ◎ ~

Hannah's life path is revealed by 2, her Date of Birth number. The numerological meanings of the number 2 (*see page 17*) show that her life path is contemplative, quiet, and supportive. Her inner personality, shown by her Birthday number, 5, is markedly different in character. The numerological meanings of the number 5 (*see page 20*) reveal that

essentially, Hannah is lively and vibrant, and has a natural inclination to flit from one area of interest to another. Although she is always exciting to be with, she is inherently unreliable.

~ ◎ ~

The considerable differences in the numerological meanings of the numbers 5 and 2 suggest that there could be deep conflict between Hannah's basic personality and her life path. However, it is equally possible that her supportive life path could be smoothing down the edges of her personality; perhaps her natural liveliness is being channeled into something useful rather than being frittered away and wasted.

~ ◎ ~

Although Hannah's life path role is contemplative and quiet, the liveliness of her 5-type basic personality means that the passivity of her 2-type life path is likely to be significantly reduced. She is therefore unlikely to allow other people to take advantage of her naturally good, gentle nature.

THE ARROWS of
PYTHAGORAS

THE ARROWS OF PYTHAGORAS ARE LINES ON A
NUMEROLOGICAL CHART. THE CHART SHOWS YOUR
MOST IMPORTANT NUMBERS, HOW THEY WORK
TOGETHER, AND THE NUMBERS THAT ARE MISSING.

The Arrows of Pythagoras grid consists of nine numbers, as shown below.

Arrows of Pythagoras grid

This is the basic Arrows of Pythagoras grid, and it shows the exact positions where your numbers should be placed. Put the numbers from your full date of birth into the corresponding squares of a blank grid. If you have any zeros in your date of birth, ignore them, because zero is considered to be an irrelevant number in numerology.

For example, John was born on February 18, 1942 (2/18/1942). Writing the numbers 2,1,8,1,9,4, and 2 in the correct positions gives the chart at the bottom of the page, known as the Date of Birth chart. The dots on the chart illustrate the missing numbers from the grid.

Everyone born in the 20th century will have at least one 1 and one 9 in their chart, and whenever you were born, there will be at least one

John's Date of Birth chart

•	•	9
22	•	8
11	4	•

square left blank. Someone born on November 11, 1911, would have seven 1s in the bottom left-hand square, and one 9.

~ 9 ~

As another example, Hannah was born on November 23, 1975 (11/23/1975). Writing the numbers 1,1,2,3,1,9,7, and 5 in the correct positions gives the Date of Birth chart shown below.

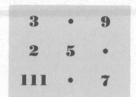

Hannah's Date of Birth chart

Once the numbers have been placed in the correct positions, draw an arrow through any columns, rows, or diagonals of three occupied squares.

~ 9 ~

John is unusual in having no lines on his Date of Birth chart whatsoever, and Hannah has three. John also has one entirely missing line, which is significant.

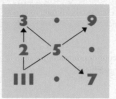

Hannah's Date of Birth chart, with the Arrows of Pythagoras

The Arrows of Pythagoras expand the understanding of John and Hannah's personalities and abilities. John has no complete lines; therefore no Arrows of Pythagoras can be drawn on his chart. He has one entirely missing line, 357. He has two numbers of the lines 123, 789, 258, 147, and 159, and therefore some propensity towards their properties (*see pages 32–33*). John only has one number of the lines 456 and 369, which shows weakness in those areas.

~ 9 ~

Hannah has three complete lines – 123, 159, and 357. Therefore three Arrows of Pythagoras can be drawn on her chart. She has some propensity toward 147, 258, 369, and 789, and is weak on 456.

INTERPRETING
THE ARROWS *of*
PYTHAGORAS

HORIZONTAL, VERTICAL, AND DIAGONAL LINES ARE
SIGNIFICANT IF THEY ARE COMPLETE, OR MISSING. IF
YOU HAVE TWO OF THE THREE NUMBERS OF A LINE,
YOU HAVE A PROPENSITY TOWARD ITS QUALITIES.

A complete 147 line reveals
that you have manual
abilities, physical dexterity,
and strength and health.
A missing 147 line points
toward impracticality
and awkwardness.

A complete 258 line reveals
that you are emotionally
balanced, artistic, and
highly sensitive. A missing
258 line points toward
emotional confusion and
oversensitivity.

GEANE

A complete 369 line reveals
that you are intelligent,
intellectual, and creative, and
that you have good judgment.
A missing 369 line points
toward dullness and poor
reasoning ability.

A complete 123 line reveals that you have good planning and organizational skills, administrative abilities, and a love of order. A missing 123 line points toward confusion, disorder, and a lack of coordination.

A complete 456 line reveals that you have strong willpower and the determination to have whatever you desire. A missing 456 line points toward frustration, disappointment, and a sense of hesitancy.

A complete 789 line reveals that you are energetic, enthusiastic, and active. A missing 789 line points toward inertia, lethargy, procrastination, laziness, and apathy.

A complete 159 line reveals that you are patient, persistent, determined, and dogged. A missing 159 line points toward a lack of motivation and purpose, resignation, and indecision.

A complete 357 line reveals that you are compassionate, spiritually aware, and serene. A missing 357 line points toward a lack of belief, and poor spiritual and emotional awareness.

TURNING YOUR NAME
into a NUMBER

NUMEROLOGY CAN EXAMINE THE ESOTERIC
NUMERICAL VALUE OF YOUR NAME. IN SOME CULTURES,
IT IS USED TO ASSESS THE CHARACTER OF A PLACE OR A
COMPANY. THE PRINCIPLE IS THE SAME IN EACH CASE.

Before the Arabic numerals (1, 2, 3, 4, 5, 6, 7, 8, 9, and 0) developed, most cultures used the letters of their alphabet to represent numbers. For example, the Roman numerals I, II, III, IV, V, VI, VII, VIII, IX, and X also belong to the Roman alphabet, and various letters from the ancient Greek and Hebrew alphabets, and Norse letter-runes, were also used as numbers.

~ ❧ ~

Modern numerology developed from the esoteric Judaism of Cabbalism, and traditionally, the Hebrew alphabet was used in numerology. Transcribing the Hebrew alphabet into the

MODERN NUMEROLOGY CONVERSION TABLE

1	2	3	4	5	6	7	8	9
A	B	C	D	E	F	G	H	I
J	K	L	M	N	O	P	Q	R
S	T	U	V	W	X	Y	Z	

Latin alphabet gave a very complicated numerological conversion table. Modern numerologists tend to place the digits 1–9 against the conventional alphabet, as shown in the table on page 34.

~ 9 ~

In the examples below, John and Hannah's names are turned to numbers by finding the numerical equivalent of the letters of their names in the Modern Numerology Conversion Table. The numbers are added together, and the digits of the total are added together until one digit remains. Turn your name to a number and see what this adds to your personality profile (*see pages 16–25*).

J O H N
1 6 8 5

$$1 + 6 + 8 + 5 = 20$$

John's Name Number

$$2 + 0 = 2$$

~ 9 ~

H A N N A H
8 1 5 5 1 8

$$8 + 1 + 5 + 5 + 1 + 8 = 28$$

$$2 + 8 = 10$$

Hannah's Name Number

$$1 + 0 = 1$$

YOUR **VOWEL**
NUMBER

IN HEBREW, VOWELS WERE NOT USUALLY WRITTEN.
CONSEQUENTLY, THEY ASSUMED A SIGNIFICANCE AS
THE SECRET PART OF YOUR NAME. THIS HIDDEN "INNER
YOU" CAN BE REVEALED BY YOUR VOWEL NUMBER.

The first name alone can be analyzed, but most numerologists examine the surname as well. Many people use a name that is different from the name assigned to them at birth. For example, Michael White might always be known as Mike White, or Marie Louise Claire Lenormand might call herself Marie-Claire Lenormand. The most used name is the name that should be numerologically analyzed.

To calculate your Vowel number, also known as the Heart number, write the full name by which you are usually known; then find the numerical equivalent of each vowel by using the Modern Numerology Conversion Table (*see page 34*). Remember that "Y" is sometimes a vowel, and sometimes a consonant. In Thierry and Yvonne "Y" is a vowel, and in Yehudi and Yolande "Y" is a consonant.

J O H N   H E R N A N D E Z
6   5   1   5

$$6 + 5 + 1 + 5 = 17$$

John's Vowel
Number

$$1 + 7 = 8$$

HANNAH DURSCHMIDT
1   1   3   9

$$1 + 1 + 3 + 9 = 14$$

Hannah's Vowel Number

$$1 + 4 = 5$$

Add the numbers together until you reach a single digit. However, if your penultimate number is 11 or 22, make a note of this, and reduce the numbers to 2 and 4 respectively.

~ෙ~

When you have calculated your Vowel number, turn to pages 16–25 to discover its meaning, and the deep "inner you." If your Vowel number is 11 (reduced to 2) or 22 (reduced to 4), look up the meanings of both numbers.

~ෙ~

John Hernandez's Vowel number is 8 (*see left*), and Hannah Durschmidt's is 5 (*see above*). John's Date of Birth number is 9 (*see pages 26–27*), and his Birthday number is also 9 (*see pages 28–29*). John's personality is ideally suited to the life path

he should follow. His Vowel number of 8 gives a clue to his achievements; essentially he is very materialistic, with the desire as well as the aptitude for making money. He might perhaps be ruthless in pursuing his ends, but he will certainly achieve them.

~ෙ~

Hannah's Date of Birth number is 2 (and 11), and her Birthday number is 5. Her Vowel number, 5, supports her Date of Birth number. The essential Hannah is lively and exciting. She is a follower rather than a leader, but her warm, energetic personality would be welcome in any team. She does not want to make leadership decisions, and is therefore unlikely to be an unstable influence on the other people in the team.

YOUR CONSONANT
NUMBER

THE CONSONANT NUMBER REVEALS THE FACE THAT
YOU SHOW TO THE OUTSIDE WORLD. IT MIGHT BE A
MASK THAT CONCEALS THE REAL YOU, OR IT MIGHT
BE AN OUTWARD PROJECTION OF WHO YOU ARE.

To calculate your Consonant number, write the name by which you are usually known, and find the numerical equivalent of each consonant by using the Modern Numerology Conversion Table (*see page 34*). Add the numbers together until you reach a single digit. However, if your penultimate numbers are 11 or 22, make a note of this, and reduce the numbers to 2 and 4 respectively.

When you have calculated your Consonant number, turn to pages 16–25 to discover the "outer you" – the external face that you present to the world. If your Consonant number was 11 (reduced to 2) or 22 (reduced to 4), look up the meanings of both numbers.

In the example below, John's Consonant number reduces to 8. His Consonant number is the same as his Vowel

J O H N   H E R N A N D E Z
1   8 5   8   9 5   5 4   8

$$1 + 8 + 5 + 8 + 9 + 5 + 5 + 4 + 8 = 53$$

John's Consonant
Number

$$5 + 3 = 8$$

HANNAH   DURSCHMIDT
8   5 5   8   4   9 1 3 8 4   4 2

$$8 + 5 + 5 + 8 + 4 + 9 + 1 +$$
$$3 + 8 + 4 + 4 + 2 = 61$$

Hannah's
Consonant Number $6 + 1 = 7$

number (*see pages 36–37*).
At its simplest, this means
that people see the "real"
John. This is usually a
positive quality, because it
means that there are no
layers of illusion or deception
between him and other
people. However, this
transparency could also cause
problems, because some
people need to have the
privacy of a secret, hidden
self, which is unknown to
the outside world.

~ᗡ~

In the example above,
Hannah's Consonant number
reduces to 7. Checking the
numerological meanings of
the number 7 (*see page 22*)
reveals that Hannah projects
herself as a loner, and not as
a teamworker. Her public
face seems to be at odds with
her private self, which was
revealed by her Vowel
number, 5. Her Date of Birth
number, 11, reduced to 2
(*see pages 26–27*), showed her
life path to be quiet and
passive, and her Consonant
number shows that she
portrays herself as reflective
and introspective. There is
no numerological conflict
between her Date of Birth
number and her Consonant
number, but perhaps Hannah
needs to separate her deep,
inner self from her public
persona. Although she has a
rich and lively inner life, she
tends to keep this to herself;
externally she appears to be
calm, cool, and quiet.

YOUR **WHOLE NAME**
NUMBER

EVERYONE IS A MIXTURE OF THEIR INNER AND OUTER
LIVES. THE WHOLE NAME NUMBER SHOWS HOW YOU
CAN RECONCILE ANY DIFFERENCES WITHIN YOURSELF
IN ORDER TO FULFIL YOUR LIFE-PLAN.

To calculate your Whole Name number, write the name by which you are usually known, and find the numerical equivalent of each letter by using the Modern Numerology Conversion Table (*see page 34*). Add the numbers together until you reach a single digit. If your penultimate numbers are 11 or 22, make a note of this, then reduce the numbers to 2 and 4 respectively. When you have calculated your Whole Name number, turn to pages 16–25 to discover the "whole you".

~ ৩ ~

John's Vowel Number (*see pages 36–37*) and Consonant number (*see pages 38–39*) are both 8, showing that he is materialistic, and his Date of Birth number (*see pages 26–27*) and Birthday number

J O H N   H E R N A N D E Z
1 6 8 5   8 5 9 5 1 5 4 5 8

**1 + 6 + 8 + 5 + 8 + 5 + 9 +
5 + 1 + 5 + 4 + 5 + 8 = 70**

John's Whole
Name Number

7 + 0 = 7

HANNAH DURSCHMIDT

8 1 5 5 1 8   4 3 9 1 3 8 4 9 4 2

$$8 + 1 + 5 + 5 + 1 + 8 + 4 + 3 + 9 +$$
$$1 + 3 + 8 + 4 + 9 + 4 + 2 = 75$$

$$7 + 5 = 12$$

Hannah's Whole Name Number

$$1 + 2 = 3$$

(*see pages 28–29*) are both 9, showing that he is an achiever. However, the example on page 40 shows that his Whole Name number is 7, suggesting introspective individuality and a highly developed intellect. This is not surprising, because there is no doubt that John is set apart from other people. He is ambitious, but he also is intelligent. It is through using his intelligence, and working as an individual, that he will achieve his goals.

Hannah's Vowel number and Birthday number are both 5, suggesting restlessness and excitement, her Date of Birth number is 2 or 11, suggesting intuition and spirituality, and her Consonant number is 7, showing that she is reflective. The example above shows that Hannah's Whole Name number is 3. It draws the restless 5 and the reflective 7 together, and shows her how she should follow her life-path. Hannah needs to be active and sociable. Although other people might perceive her as being aloof, she can overcome their perceptions by deliberately pursuing the interesting life-path of a 3-type person.

YOUR NAME &
THE ARROWS *of* PYTHAGORAS

THE DISTRIBUTION OF THE INDIVIDUAL LETTERS IN
YOUR NAME IS AS SIGNIFICANT IN NUMEROLOGY AS THE
SUM. THIS DISTRIBUTION CAN BE ANOTHER VALUABLE
CLUE TO YOUR STRENGTHS AND WEAKNESSES.

Write the name by which you are usually known, and find the numerical equivalent of each letter by using the Modern Numerology Conversion Table (*see page 34*). Next, enter the numbers into the appropriate squares in a blank Arrows of Pythagoras grid (*see page 30*). The number of letters entered

will be determined by the length of your name – Frederick Barbarossa has many more letters than Jane Gray, for example – but the numerical equivalents even out the distribution.

~ ⁹ ~

When you have entered your numbers into the grid, turn to the interpretations on pages 32–33 to see what the

J O H N   H E R N A N D E Z
1 6 8 5   8 5 9 5 1 5 4 5 8

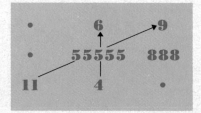

**John's Whole
Name Chart**

HANNAH   DURSCHMIDT
8 1 5 5 1 8   4 3 9 1 3 8 4 9 4 2

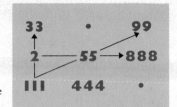

Hannah's Whole Name Chart

strong, weak, complete, or missing lines indicate about your character.

~⑨~

The example on page 42 shows that John has the 159 diagonal, which shows determination. He also has 456, indicating willpower, and the determination to have whatever he desires. Although he has no completely missing lines, he is weak on 123 (planning and organizational skills) and on 357 (compassion and understanding the needs of others). His weakness on 357 is not surprising, considering his materialistic nature and strong determination to achieve his ends, and the 357 line was also missing

from the Arrows of Pythagoras on his Date of Birth chart (*see pages 30–31*).

~⑨~

The example above shows that Hannah has the lines 159 (dogged determination), 123 (organizational skills), and 258 (emotional balance and sensitivity). She is fairly strong (two out of three numbers present) on every other line. Hannah has no weak lines or missing lines. On her Date of Birth chart, Hannah also had 159 and 123, showing that these are major characteristics in her personality. The partial 258 line on that chart is strengthened by the complete line in this Arrows of Pythagoras Name chart.

PUTTING YOUR
DATE & NAME TOGETHER

IN NUMEROLOGY, IF YOU PUT YOUR DATE OF BIRTH
AND YOUR WHOLE NAME TOGETHER, IT CAN GIVE A
VERY FULL PICTURE OF YOUR PERSONALITY, AS WELL AS
YOUR STRENGTHS AND WEAKNESSES.

Superimpose your Date of Birth chart (*see pages 30–31*) onto your Whole Name chart (*see pages 42–43*). They should reinforce each other. Some numbers might be strengthened by their presence in both charts, and gaps in one chart could be filled in by the other. The extra numbers should fill the chart. Therefore, what is missing becomes more significant than what is present, both in individual numbers and in lines. Turn to the interpretations of the Arrows of Pythagoras (*see pages 32–33*) to discover what the strong, weak, complete, or missing lines indicate about your character.

DATE OF BIRTH 2/18/1942

J O H N   H E R N A N D E Z
1 6 8 5   8 5 9 5 5 1 5 4 5 8

John's
Combined
Chart

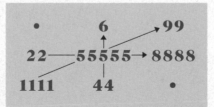

HANNAH DURSCHMIDT

8 1 5 5 1 8   4 3 9 1 3 8 4 9 4 2

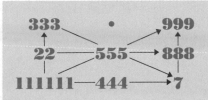

Hannah's
Combined
Chart

Superimposing John's Date of Birth chart onto his Whole Name chart gives the example on page 44. It shows that even with a combined chart, John has only three Arrows of Pythagoras. The extra numbers involved in superimposing one chart onto another suggest that any incomplete line is a weak line. Therefore, John is weak on 147 (physical strength and health), 369 (judgment), 123 (order and planning), 789 (activity), and particularly weak on 357 (compassion and spiritual awareness). Lack of spiritual and emotional understanding and compassion can easily lead to lack of serenity, and John must pay serious attention to these areas.

～⑨～

The example above shows that Hannah is only missing one number – 6 – from her combined chart. As a result, she has six complete Arrows of Pythagoras, and two incomplete ones – 369 and 456. A weak 369 suggests mental dullness rather than a lack of intelligence; perhaps she has a poor memory, or is slow to grasp complex arguments. The weak 456 suggests too much hesitancy in Hannah, which could cause her to miss some important opportunities.

MISSING
NUMBERS

EXAMINE ALL THE NUMBERS THAT YOU HAVE
CALCULATED, AND SEE IF ANY ARE MISSING. IT IS
BETTER TO HAVE A BALANCE OF DIFFERENT NUMBERS
THAN TO HAVE CONCENTRATIONS OF JUST A FEW.

Look at your combined chart (*see pages 44–45*), and see which, if any, numbers are missing. If you do have missing numbers, see if you can find any of them among your five personality numbers – your Date of Birth number (*see pages 26–27*), Birthday number (*see pages 28–29*), Vowel number (*see pages 36–37*), Consonant number (*see pages 38–39*), and Whole Name number (*see pages 40–41*).

Check your five personality numbers; if any numbers are still missing, turn to pages 16–25 and look up the meanings of the missing numbers. The numbers that are missing from your charts represent the areas of your personality that might need some attention.

For example, John was missing the numbers 3 and 7 from his combined chart, and his five personality numbers are shown below.

John's Whole Name number adds a reflective 7, but 3 is still missing from his

John's Personality Numbers

DATE OF BIRTH NUMBER	**9**
BIRTHDAY NUMBER	**9**
VOWEL NUMBER	**8**
CONSONANT NUMBER	**8**
WHOLE NAME NUMBER	**7**

numerological profile. This denotes a serious weakness in the areas of creativity, versatility, and sociability. Failing to communicate well with other people could stop him from achieving his goals; missing out on social enjoyment is a sad lack in his life. John probably takes himself too seriously, and it would undoubtedly be beneficial for him to have some fun in his life.

~ 9 ~

Hannah was only missing one number from her combined grid – 6 – and her five personality numbers are shown above.

~ 9 ~

Hannah's Consonant number – 7 – strengthens the single 7 on her combined chart, and fortunately she does not add any more 1s to the six that she already has; too many of any number can cause an imbalance.

~ 9 ~

The number 6 is completely missing from Hannah's numbers, which shows a surprising lack of supportive and nurturing qualities. Hannah needs to concentrate

DATE OF BIRTH NUMBER	2
BIRTHDAY NUMBER	5
VOWEL NUMBER	5
CONSONANT NUMBER	7
WHOLE NAME NUMBER	3

Hannah's Personality Numbers

on improving her sense of responsibility for other people. This should make her personality more "rounded," and add to her sense of fulfillment with life.

~ 9 ~

Do not worry if you have one or more missing numbers in your numerological profile. Numerology does not reveal how you are destined to be – it helps to identify your strengths and weaknesses instead. Study the number meanings (*see pages 16–25*) and try to develop the character traits and abilities that you lack most.

CHANGING
YOUR NAME

YOUR DATE OF BIRTH CANNOT BE CHANGED, BUT YOU
CAN CHANGE YOUR NAME. CHANGING YOUR NAME IS
LIKELY TO HAVE A NUMEROLOGICAL EFFECT BY ALSO
CHANGING YOUR PERSONALITY NUMBERS.

In many cultures it has been traditional for a woman to take her husband's surname when they marry. Some numerologists believe that over a certain period of time, the personality might change to suit the new name. People change their names for a variety of other reasons. It could be a personal tribute to someone they love and admire; an attempt to distance themselves from their family; a new, professional working name for a performer, or sometimes simply because they feel their name is not right for them.

SIMPLY SIX
*The US boxer
Cassius Clay
changed his name to
Muhammad Ali in
1964. This changed
his Vowel number
from 5 to 6, and his
Consonant number
from 1 to 9, but his
Whole Name number
remained unchanged
at the harmonious,
well-balanced 6.*

FOR BETTER OR WORSE
It has been traditional for a woman to take her husband's name when they marry. A change of name usually affects the numerological analysis.

Many people are known by a variant of their first name. Charles, for example, might be known as Charlie, Chuck, or Chas, and Elizabeth might be known as Liz, Beth, or Betty. If someone who used to be known as Susan prefers the name Sue, and if her friends refer to her as Sue, then Sue is the name that should be analyzed, not Susan.

Perhaps it might seem as if you are "cheating" if you change your name or its spelling simply to have a positive affect on its numerological analysis. However, if you are planning to change your name anyway, check the implications first.

Calculate your Vowel number (*see pages 36–37*), Consonant number (*see pages 38–39*), and Whole Name number (*see pages 40–41*) for different versions of your first name. See if your missing numbers now occur, but also check which numbers you lose.

THE NUMEROLOGY *of* YEARS

IF YOUR DATE OF BIRTH CAN PROVIDE INFORMATION
ABOUT YOUR PERSONALITY, IT SHOULD BE POSSIBLE TO
USE DATES TO LOOK AHEAD AND PREDICT WHAT
FUTURE YEARS MIGHT BRING FOR YOU.

Numerologists believe that individual years, decades, and centuries have their own characters. The meanings of numbers (*see pages 16–25*) always remain the same, whether it is birth dates, names, or years that are being analyzed.

Numerologically reducing years to a single number can be used as a prediction for those years. For example, 1997, 1998, and 1999 can be reduced as shown opposite. The number 8 is concerned with materialism and worldly matters. The year 1997 is therefore associated with business, and with making money, or losing it; 8 is often associated with failure. The number 9 is powerful, and suggests completion and achievement. Consequently,

$$1 + 9 + 9 + 7 = 26$$

$$2 + 6 = 8$$

1997

$$1 + 9 + 9 + 8 = 27$$

$$2 + 7 = 9$$

1998

$$1 + 9 + 9 + 9 = 28$$

$$2 + 8 = 10$$

$$1 + 0 = 1$$

1999

$$2 + 1 + 8 + 1 + 9 + 9 + 8 = 38$$

$$3 + 8 = 11$$

$$1 + 1 = 2$$

John and 1998

1998 is likely to be a year of brilliance and fulfillment, particularly in the artistic sphere. The number 1 is associated with new beginnings, mental powers, and leadership. The year 1999 could therefore be a time of major new projects, and of great achievement.

~ 9 ~

The numerology of years can also be used for predictions. Add the day and month of your birth to any other year, to see how the characteristics of that year will affect you. For example, adding John's month of birth (2) and day of birth (18) to the year 1998

gives the reduced number 2. This shows that 1998 should be a passive year for John. This does not necessarily mean a lack of achievement; perhaps passivity will prove more effective than assertion.

~ 9 ~

The example below adds Hannah's month of birth (11) and her day of birth (23) to the year 1997. The reduced number – 6 – shows that 1997 is likely to be a good year for home building and material comfort. This number was missing from Hannah's profile, but in 1997 she might be able to add this aspect to her life.

$$1 + 1 + 2 + 3 + 1 + 9 + 9 + 7 = 33$$

$$3 + 3 = 6$$

Hannah and 1997

OTHER USES *of* NUMBERS: SQUARES

FOR CENTURIES, SYMBOLS SUCH AS LETTERS AND
NUMBERS HAVE BEEN USED TO REPRESENT LANGUAGE
AND COUNTING. THEY HAVE ALSO BEEN LAID OUT TO
MAGICAL EFFECT IN A VARIETY OF WAYS.

The existence of number squares has been noted since Pythagorean times. For example, all the numbers from 1 to 9 can be put in a 3-square grid, so that the total of each line – vertical, horizontal, or diagonal – is 15. The total of the square is 45 (3 x 15). Similarly, a 4-square grid containing all the numbers from 1 to 16 can be designed so that each line of the grid totals 34. The total of the square is 136 (4 x 34).

3-square Grid

4	9	2
3	5	7
8	1	6

The ancients ascribed each differently numbered grid to an astrological planet and to a color. For example, a 3-square grid was associated with the planet Saturn and the color black, and a 4-square grid was associated with Jupiter and orange.

Magic word squares, or other designs using arrangements of letters, were often used as amulets against evil. The most famous word of magic, Abracadabra, probably derived from the deity Abraxas. The philosopher Basilides (AD 85–145) set up an esoteric school in Alexandria. He taught that there was a supreme, transcendent god, Abraxas, who had a human body, the head of a hawk, and legs of serpents. In the Greek system of numerology, the name Abraxas adds up to 365, the number of days in a year, and the number of heavens in Basilides' cosmology. According to Basilides, the number 365 contained considerable magic power, which could make anyone invincible. Abracadabra was originally used to ward off fevers.

Acronyms have also had esoteric meanings for centuries. Instead of the cross, the early Christians used the sign of the fish as their secret symbol. The Greek word for fish, ICHTHYS, represents the first letters of the Greek words for "Jesus Christ, Son of God, Saviour".

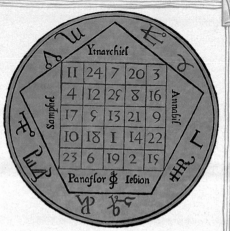

MAGIC MARS
This seal shows the magic square of Mars. Each line of this five-square grid totals 65, and the whole grid totals 365 (5 x 65). As its name suggests, it is associated with the planet Mars, and the colour red.

```
A B R A C A D A B R A
  B R A C A D A B R
    R A C A D A B
      A C A D A
        C A D
          A
```

Abracadabra Magic Word Amulet

OTHER USES *of* NUMBERS: ESOTERIC SYSTEMS

THE ESOTERIC MEANINGS OF THE SIGNIFICANT NUMBERS IN NUMEROLOGY HAVE STRONG LINKS WITH MANY OTHER METAPHYSICAL, MAGICAL, AND DIVINATORY SYSTEMS.

Numerology has its roots in Cabbalism, the esoteric strand of Judaism. This complex system is centered on the Tree of Life, which uses ten points on the tree, and the 22 pathways that link them, to illustrate man's relationship with God. Each pathway is numbered with one of the 22 letters of the Hebrew alphabet.

Tarot also has links with Cabbalism. The 19th-century esotericists Etteilla, Eliphas Lévi, and Papus linked the 22 pathways of the Tree of Life with the 22 cards of the Tarot's Major Arcana. The early 20th-century British occult society, the Hermetic Order of the Golden Dawn, made Tarot correspond with

TAROT AND NUMEROLOGY
A mystical relationship with Cabbalism, the esoteric strand of Judaism, is shared by numerology and Tarot. This Fool and the Five of Cups are from the Spanish Tarot.

I CHING CARDS

Cards can be used to consult the I Ching. These two cards illustrate the meaning of the trigrams, which make up the hexagrams at the bottoms of the cards.

the Cabbalah even more closely by placing the Fool before Card 1 instead of before Card 21, and swapping Justice and Fortitude, Cards 8 and 11.

CASTING COINS
These I Ching coins have a yang side and a yin side. Yang includes the concepts light and male, and yin includes the concepts dark and female.

The Chinese divinatory system, the I Ching, is based on complementary opposites, called yang and yin. It takes a solid line to represent yang, and a broken line to represent yin, and builds eight possible sets of three lines, called trigrams. Placing any trigram on top of another gives the 64 hexagrams of the I Ching, and each hexagram has its own meaning.

OTHER USES *of* NUMBERS:
MUSIC

RHYTHM, MELODY, AND HARMONY ARE COMPLETELY
DEPENDENT ON NUMBERS. MUSIC IS VERY POWERFUL IN
MYSTICAL AND MAGICAL TERMS, AND IN TERMS OF
YOUR OWN PERSONAL DEVELOPMENT.

Music is one of the oldest areas of human life. Virtually everyone listens to it, and everyone owns a musical instrument – the human voice. Music is a universal language.

Pythagoras (*see pages 12–13*) calculated the principles of the musical octave, and the intervals between notes of a scale, on a mathematical basis. Harmonics, the "hidden" notes of a stringed instrument, can be heard when you touch a plucked string at a half, third, or quarter of its length. Musical intervals such as a perfect third or a perfect fifth could be called aural representations of mathematical statements.

The very earliest music was purely rhythmic – the beating of a drum, and rhythm is a manipulation of numbers. From primitive rituals to rock festivals, dancing depends on the rhythm of the drums. Armies march to a drum beat; apart from keeping the soldiers in step, the repetitive rhythm raises their courage and spirits. In some tribal societies drums are used to send messages, and the artificial rhythms of the Morse code are an extension of the same principle.

**RATTLE
AND DRUM**
*As its name suggests,
this Indian rattle drum is
half drum and half rattle.*

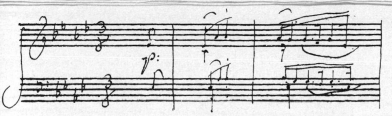

NOTATING NOTES
The complex numerical information in a single sheet of music includes the number of beats in the bar and the length of the notes.

Music can have a magical effect on both performers and listeners. It is highly emotive, and can be uplifting, soothing, or saddening – sometimes all at once. Throughout history, scholars and philosophers have linked music with both mysticism and magic – for example, esoteric scholars Pythagoras, Plato (*c.* 428–*c.* 348 BC), and Plutarch (*c.* 46–120 BC), Hermetic philosophers Robert Fludd (1574–1637) and Johannes Kepler (1571–1630), the founder of the mystical philosophy, anthroposophy, Rudolf Steiner (1861–1925), and one of the most significant modern writers on the esoteric, R. J. Stewart.

Try a personal experiment in music appreciation. From the music that you might enjoy, select the one piece that expresses the esoteric meaning of each of the numbers (*see pages 16–25*). If you are trying to develop any of the qualities associated with the numbers, play that particular piece of music while you meditate.

57

SOUNDS FISHY
This fish-shaped stringed instrument is a rajao, a 19th-century Portuguese lute with five strings.

OTHER USES *of* NUMBERS:
COLORS

NUMBERS AND COLORS HAVE CERTAIN ASSOCIATIONS.
WHEN YOUR EYES PERCEIVE FREQUENCIES OF LIGHT
WAVES YOU SEE COLORS, AND FREQUENCIES DEPEND ON
NUMERICAL RELATIONSHIPS.

Colors have different emotional effects. Red, for example, is an aggressive, dangerous color, green is gentle and calming, and blue is cool and intellectually stimulating. The shade of the color is also important. A soft rose-colored living room, for example, suggests the controlled warmth of a fireside. The color of your clothing can have a personal effect – wearing a clean shade of blue might make you feel cool and sophisticated, and bright red might show that you are feeling aggressive, literally "fiery," or passionate.

Numerology can help you to identify the colors that match your personality. Look at your Date of Birth number (*see pages 26–27*), Birthday number (*see pages 28–29*), Vowel number (*see pages 36–37*), Consonant number (*see pages 38–39*), and Whole Name number (*see pages 40–41*). If one number recurs more than the others, or if you consider a number's meaning (*see pages 16–25*) to be the "real you," then it is likely that the associated colors will match your personality.

1 Amber

2 Pearl

3 Amethyst

Emphasize the "inner you" by wearing colors or gemstones that match your Vowel number, or encourage your life path by wearing colors or gemstones that are linked with your Date of Birth number. Accentuate the qualities of your numbers by wearing the associated colors or gemstones.

Sapphire

5

Diamond

~~~ ⦾ ~~~

Number 1 is associated with the colors yellow, orange, and gold, and the gemstones topaz and amber. Number 2 is associated with the colors green, cream, and white, and the gemstones moonstone, pearl, and jade. Number 3 is associated with the colors mauve, violet, and pale purple, and with the gemstone amethyst.

~~~ ⦾ ~~~

Number 4 is associated with the colors blue, gray, and silver, and the gemstone sapphire. Number 5 is associated with pastel shades of all colors and the gemstone diamond. Number 6

is associated with most shades of blue and turquoise, and the gemstone emerald.

6

Emerald

~~~ ⦾ ~~~

Number 7 is associated with the colors green, yellow, and gold, and the gemstones pearl, moonstone, and cats'-eye. Number 8 is associated with dark shades of gray, purple, blue, black, and the gemstones black pearl and dark sapphire. Number 9 is associated with most shades of red, and the gemstones garnet, ruby, and bloodstone.

7

Moonstone

9

Garnet

8

Dark Sapphire

INDEX

Abracadabra, 52, 53
Abraxas, 52, 53
Agrippa, Henry
    Cornelius, 11
Arrows of Pythagoras,
    the, 30–31, 32–33
Aristotle, 13
Ashmole, Elias, 11

Balliett, L. Dow, 11
Basilides, 52, 53
Birthday number, 28–29

Cabbalism, 10
California Institute of
    Numerical Research,
    the, 11
Combined chart, 44–45
Consonant number,
    38–39

Date of Birth chart, 30,
    31
Date of Birth number,
    26–27
"David," 14
Dee, John, 11
dice, 8

eight, 23
eleven, 25

five, 20
Fludd, Robert, 11, 57
four, 19
four-square grid, 52

Hermetic philosophers,
    the, 10, 11, 57

I Ching, the, 55

Kepler, Johannes, 57

magic word squares, 52
Michelangelo, 14
Modern Numerology
    Conversion Table,
    34, 35

Name number, 35

nine, 24
Noah's Ark, 8
number squares, 52–53

Old Testament, the, 8
one, 16

Personality numbers,
    46, 47
Plato, 13, 57
Plutarch, 57
Pythagoras, 12–13, 57

Rosicrucians, the, 8

seven, 22
six, 21
Solomon's Temple, 8
Steiner, Rudolf, 57
Stewart, R. J., 57

Tarot, 54
three, 18
three-square grid, 52
Tree of Life, the, 10, 54
twelve, 9
twenty-two, 25
two, 17

"Venus de Milo," the,
    15
Vowel number, 36–37

Whole Name chart, 42,
    43
Whole Name number,
    40–41

years, numerology of,
    50, 51

zero, 15, 30

ACKNOWLEDGMENTS

Artworks
John Beech 4, 5, 14, 15, 16, 17,
18, 19, 20, 21, 22, 23, 24, 25;
Anna Benjamin

Special Photography
Steve Gorton and Tim Ridley

Additional Photography
Jane Burton, Philip Dowell, Colin Keates,
Dave King, Harry Taylor.

Editorial assistance Martha Swift,
Picture research assistance Ingrid Nilsson
DTP design assistance Daniel McCarthy.

The publisher would like to thank the following for
their kind permission to reproduce material:

The Aquarian Press, HarperCollins Publishers,
77-85 Fulham Palace Road, Hammersmith, London W6 8JB:
The I Ching Card Pack by Anthony Clark and Richard Gill;
Naipes Heraclio Fournier, P.O. Box 94, Vitoria, Spain: *Spanish Tarot.*

Picture Credits

Key: *t* top; *c* center; *b* below; *l* left; *r* right

AKG/Galleria dell' Accademia Firenze 14*bl*/Musee du Louvre Paris 15*tr*;
Jean-Loup Charmet 8*bl*; Mary Evans Picture Library 12*bl*, 57*tr*;
Image Bank 49*tr*; Images Color Library 9*tr*, 10*bl*, 11*tr*, 22*br*, 53*tr*;
Rex Features Ltd 48*bl*; Harry Smith Collection 18*tr*.